COUNTRY FOOD

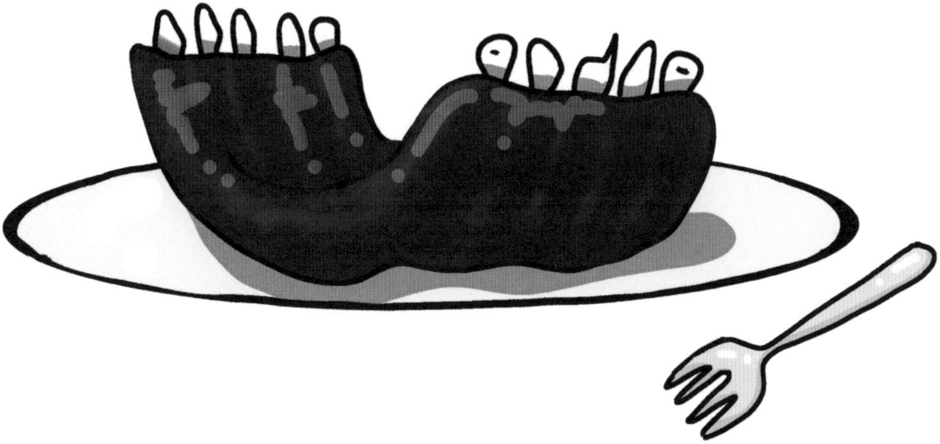

ILLUSTRATED BY

Aija Aiofe Komangapik

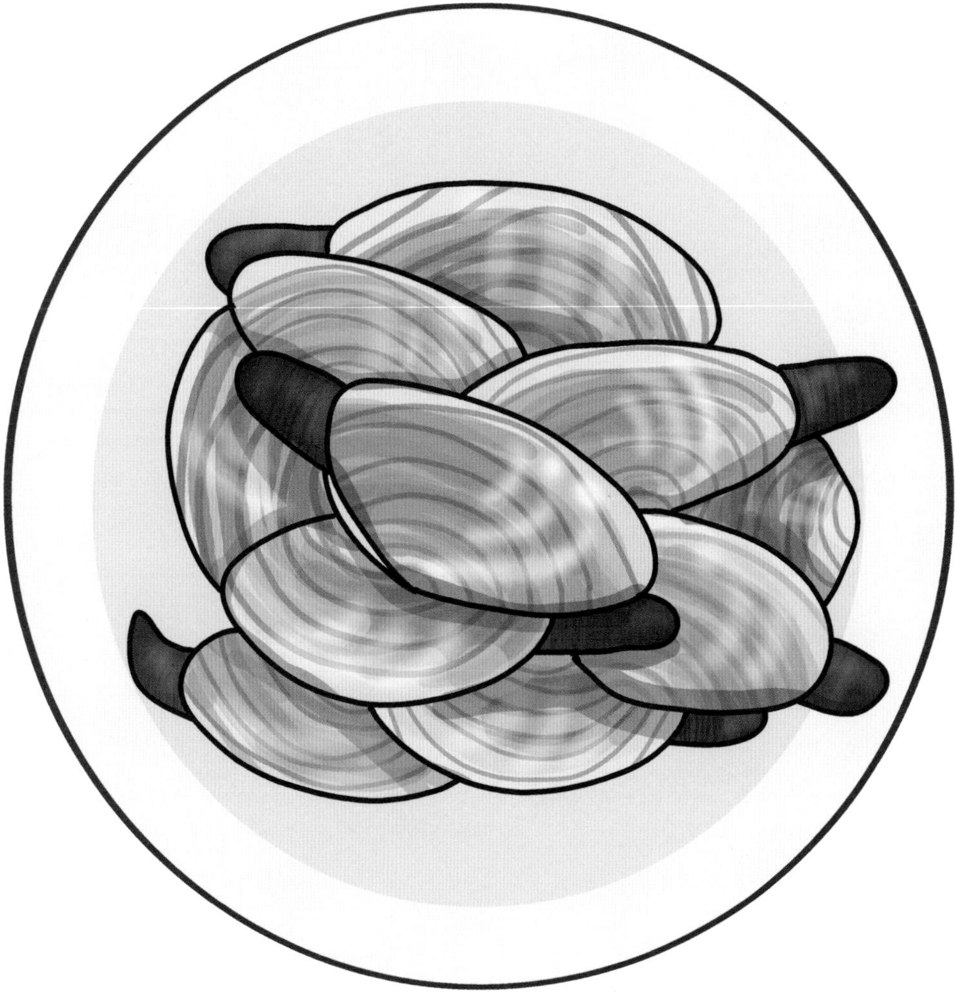

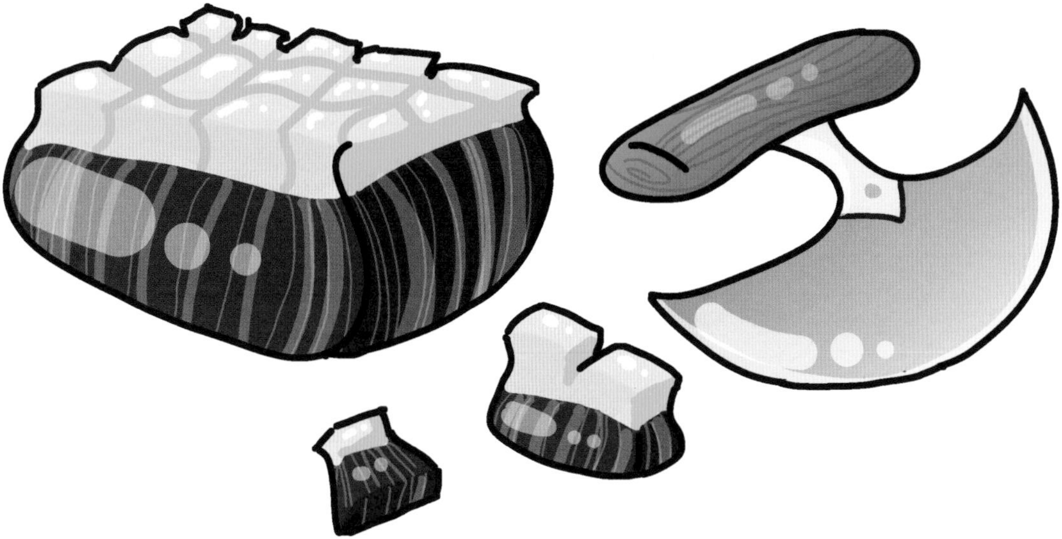

pitsi

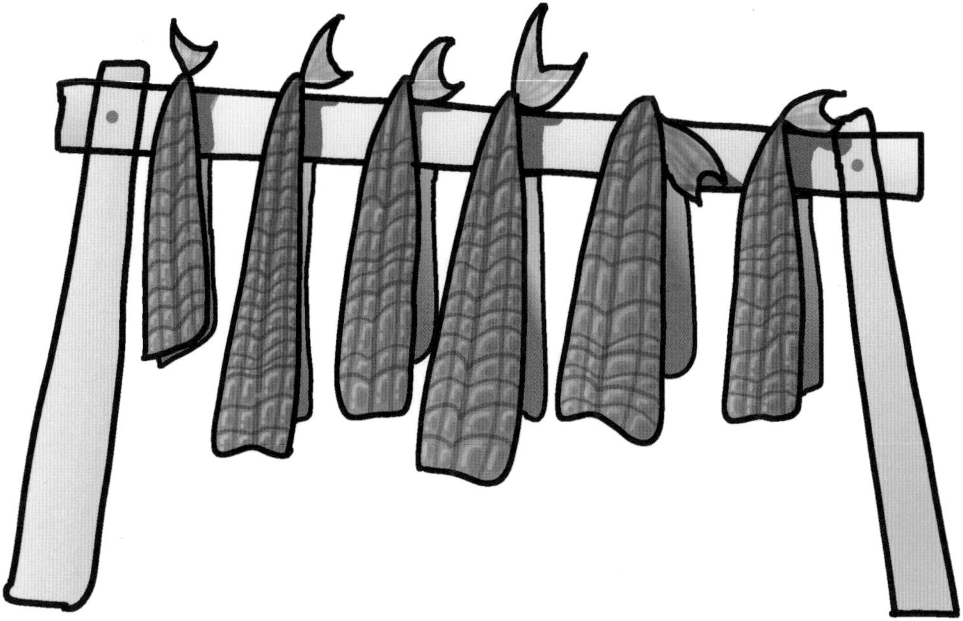

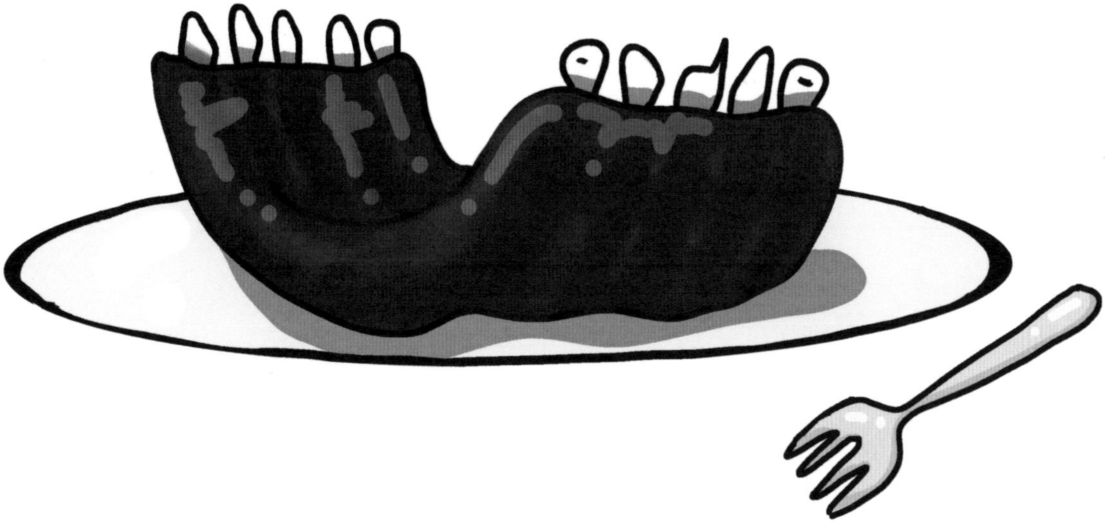

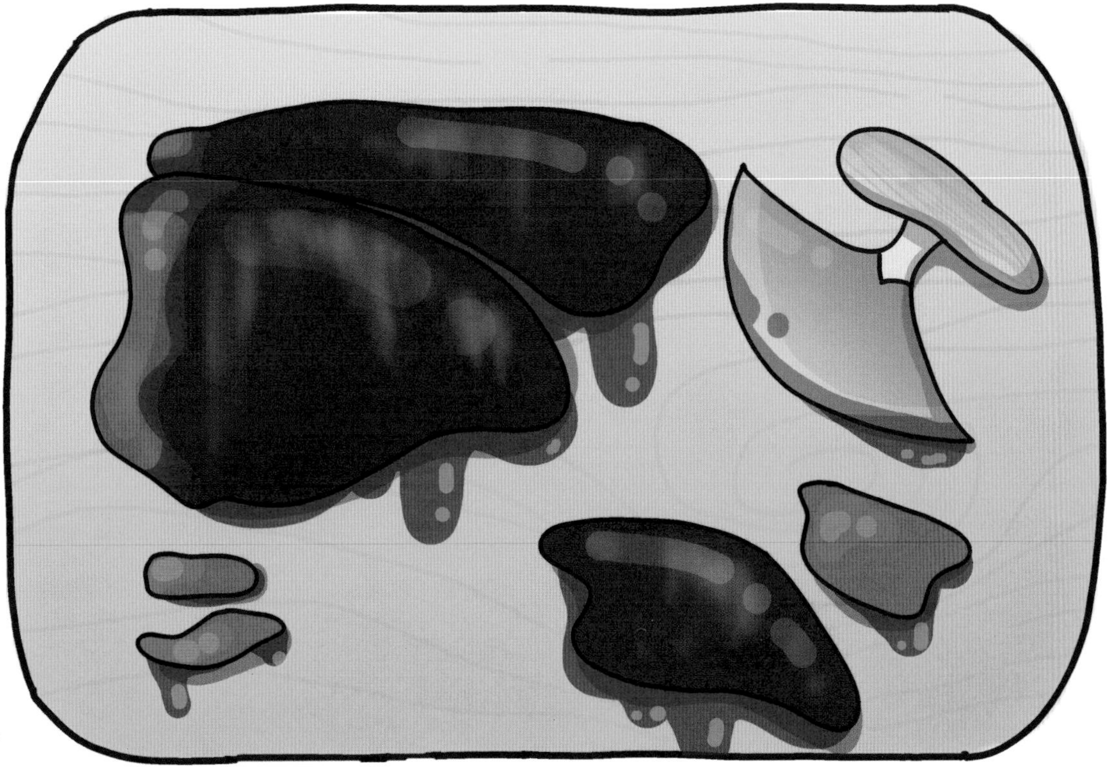

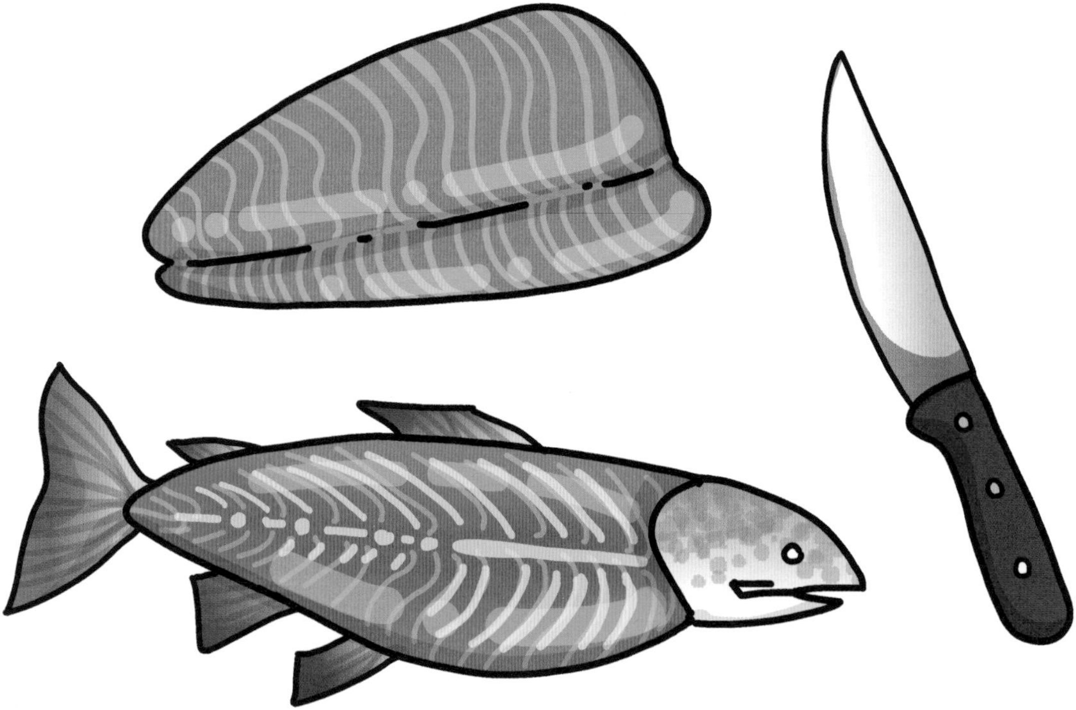

fish